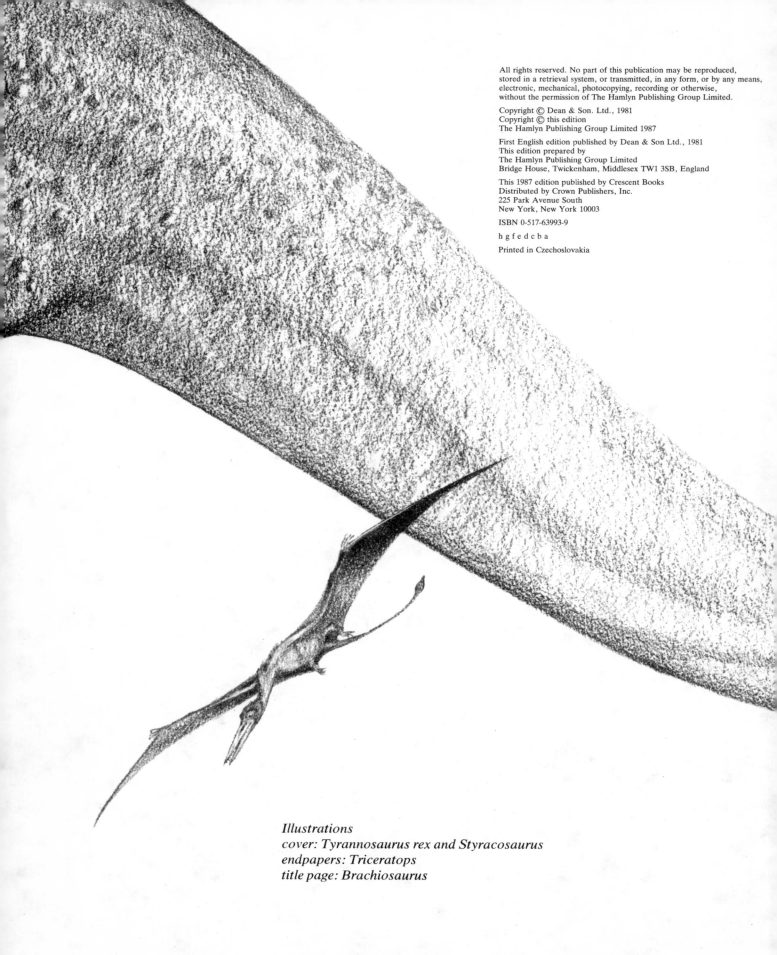

Copyright © Dean & Son. Ltd., 1981
Copyright © this edition
The Hamlyn Publishing Group Limited 1987

First English edition published by Dean & Son Ltd., 1981
This edition prepared by
The Hamlyn Publishing Group Limited
Bridge House, Twickenham, Middlesex TW1 3SB, England

This 1987 edition published by Crescent Books
Distributed by Crown Publishers, Inc.
225 Park Avenue South
New York, New York 10003

ISBN 0-517-63993-9

h g f e d c b a

Printed in Czechoslovakia

Illustrations
cover: Tyrannosaurus rex and Styracosaurus
endpapers: Triceratops
title page: Brachiosaurus

THE AMAZING WORLD OF
DINOSAURS

Written and illustrated by
Terry Riley

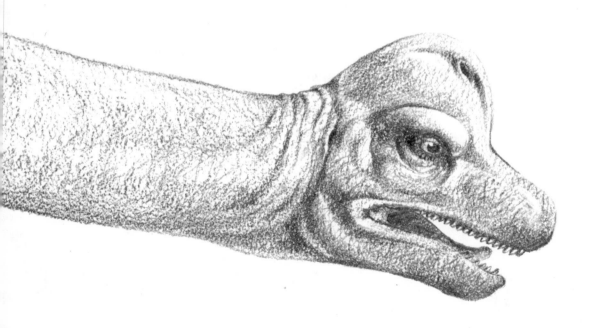

Crescent Books
New York

IN SEARCH OF DINOSAURS

Just two centuries ago, nobody knew that the dinosaurs and other huge prehistoric reptiles had even existed. Our knowledge of these creatures comes from the fossilized remains which scientists have excavated and studied. One of the first fossils of a large reptile to be found was that of an Ichthyosaur. This was found by a twelve-year-old British girl, Mary Anning, in 1811. She later discovered fossils of two more extinct reptiles, those of a Plesiosaur and a Pterodactyl.

Mary Anning's marvellous discoveries were made in the limestone rocks of Dorset. Since then, dinosaur remains have been excavated all over the world. Most dinosaur remains are found in rock formations that were once mud at the bottom of ancient seas, rivers and lakes. The mud gradually hardened into rocks, preserving the remains of any creatures that were buried in the mud. Slowly the oceans and lakes receded and disappeared, and the rocks formed beneath them became dry land. The weather wore away the rocks, eventually exposing the preserved remains of the animals entombed within.

These remains are called fossils. Each type of rock produces different kinds of fossils, because each was originally part of a different environment. Therefore marine deposits, from which limestone formed, reveal fossils of ancient sea creatures. Rocks such as sandstone and shale, which formed from the mud of rivers, estuaries and lakes, produce fossils of the inhabitants of forests, plains and marshes. The bones of dinosaurs are not the only traces of these creatures of long ago. Their footprints and even their eggs have also been found preserved. Finds have also revealed the skin texture of some dinosaurs, as well as the fossilized remains of bony plates which armoured their backs.

Sometimes only part of a long-dead creature is found, such as the forearms of Deinocheirus. The arms measure 2.5 metres (8 feet) long and end in enormous claws, showing it to be possibly one of the most terrifying flesh eaters of its time. Its name in fact means 'terrible hand'. Perhaps one day more remains of this dinosaur will be found, and we shall then see if this creature really was as formidable as its arms make it appear.

New discoveries sometimes mean that the history books, at least in part, have to be rewritten for new specimens occasionally reveal previously unknown features. All reptiles alive at the time of the dinosaurs were thought to be cold-blooded animals, just like today's reptiles. Then a complete fossilized Pterosaur discovered in 1971 showed that these creatures were covered in fur. Pterosaurs would only have needed fur if they were warm-blooded. Pterosaurs are now regarded as having been a special group of warm-blooded reptiles, though some think they should not be thought of as reptiles at all but placed in a separate group.

Dinosaurs ruled the earth in a time known as the Mesozoic Era. This lasted from 225 million to 65 million years ago, and is usually split into three periods. The first is the Triassic period, next comes the Jurassic period and finally the Cretaceous period, at the end of which all the dinosaurs mysteriously vanished from the face of the earth.

The arm of Deinocheirus compared with a man.

DEATH OF THE DINOSAURS

The disappearance of the dinosaurs is one of nature's great mysteries. While scientists are able to reconstruct the true appearance of dinosaurs, because of various clues in their bone structure and from other evidence, the death of the dinosaurs is still a matter of conjecture and controversy. There are many theories and many schools of thought, but we do not in fact know what caused the extinction of these highly successful creatures.

Some scientists believe that a world-wide onset of cold weather, a sort of mini ice-age, caused the dinosaurs to die out. This would undoubtedly have been fatal if all the dinosaurs had been huge cold-blooded reptiles, for reptiles need a continual supply of heat from the sun to warm their bodies in order to become active. The strange thing is that not only the huge land-living reptiles disappeared but also the fur-covered reptiles, such as Pterosaurs, and many of the marine animals of the time also became extinct. If we are to subscribe to the theory of sudden cold, we must ask ourselves how the smaller reptiles such as turtles and crocodiles and other creatures managed to survive this period and remain almost unchanged into our times.

This great tragedy for the giant animals of the distant past was probably mankind's greatest blessing. Had the dinosaurs continued to rule the earth, then the mammals may not have risen to their present-day dominance of the animal world. This would have meant that the evolutionary chain of events leading to the appearance of man may well have not occurred. In the days of the dinosaurs, mammals played only a minor role in the nature of things and so an opportunity to advance might not otherwise have happened.

As new evidence comes to light on the lives of the dinosaurs, perhaps one day an answer to the mystery of their death will be found.

Protoceratops

Adverse weather conditions may have killed many dinosaurs.

THE WORLD OF DINOSAURS

Dinosaurs began their rise to fame in the Triassic period about 200 million years ago. This was a time when both plants and animals became more diverse as they took advantage of the many new environments that had begun to develop. Some of the creatures of this ancient era, such as crocodiles and turtles, became so well adapted to their surroundings that they evolved no further and remain unchanged even now.

One particular group of animals emerged from the Triassic to become the dominant animals on earth. These were the dinosaurs, most of which were reptiles. They ruled the earth for more than 100 million years, an enormous span of time. Their eventual extinction allowed the mammals to rise from obscurity and then they in their turn evolved and came to produce a new ruler of the earth—man. So far, his dominance has lasted only a few thousand years—a brief moment in comparison to the long, long reign of the dinosaurs.

When the ancestors of the dinosaurs began to establish themselves in the Triassic landscapes, the climate was very dry. Most plant life was found only in places that promised a good supply of moisture, such as swamps and lakes, and it was in such locations that many of the first dinosaurs lived and developed. The dry, arid conditions of the Triassic eventually gave way to a period of wetter and warmer weather, the Jurassic. This period lasted from 195 million years ago to 135 million years ago. Its ideal growing conditions gave rise to more luxuriant and diverse vegetation. Conifer trees and the palm-like cycads grew abundantly, and many areas had thick undergrowths of fern. This was a time when huge forests began to spread over the land, and they contained several trees that are familiar to us today, such as the yew and the cypress.

There were many huge marshy areas and fresh-water lakes, inhabited not only by dinosaurs but by the first frogs and other amphibious creatures.

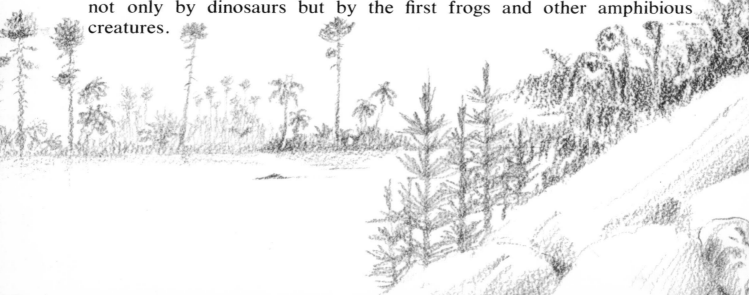

Here too lived the early mammals, and other mammal-like creatures which evolved and became extinct before man's time on earth.

The third period of the Mesozoic Era—the Cretaceous—is the period during which the dinosaurs reached their evolutionary peak, and at the end of which they ceased to exist. The Cretaceous period began 135 million years ago, and lasted for about 60 million years. It is marked by the rule of the dinosaurs, but it was also a time when most of the trees and flowers that flourish today became established. Therefore dinosaurs lived and roamed in forests, grasslands and other habitats that would look familiar to us today. Birds sang in trees, and bees searched blossoms for pollen. Butterflies and moths flitted through sunlit glades pollinating flowers, just as they do today. But one thing missing from this apparently modern landscape was any kind of large mammal, for this was the time when the dinosaurs reigned supreme.

The ancestors of the dinosaurs and of modern reptiles were all small lizard-like creatures. But as time passed, these animals produced larger animals and eventually gave rise to heavily-built reptiles like Shansisuchus and the earliest crocodiles. The first true dinosaur to appear was Ornithosuchus. It was a 3 metre (10 feet) long flesh eater, the first of the large flesh-eating dinosaurs or carnosaurs. Another early dinosaur was Thecodontosaurus, an animal also 3 metres (10 feet) in length that ate plants as well as flesh. This type of dinosaur belonged to a group that developed into the largest animals that have ever walked the earth, the plant-eating dinosaurs known as Sauropods.

Another group of animals began to take to the air, the Pterosaurs. At first they were merely gliders but as time passed, they evolved into true fliers. The sea became the domain of the reptiles and many varieties found a home there, including the Ichthyosaurs or fish lizards. The shore lines of the ancient oceans also had their own particular inhabitants, and it was in such localities that many types of ancient crocodiles flourished. Slowly but surely, the reptiles began to dominate the land, sea and air. By the Jurassic period, a pattern had been set and they were firmly established. Their rule would last for more than 100 million years.

Below: Shansisuchus, an ancient Archosaur. Opposite: Dimorphodon, a Pterosaur.

The ancient seas

In the days of the dinosaurs, marine life was in many respects similar to that of today. But although fishes, squids, molluscs and jellyfish lived in the oceans, mammals such as dolphins, whales and seals were absent. The reptiles reigned supreme. The dominant sea-going predators of the day belonged to three main groups—the Ichthyosaurs, Plesiosaurs and, late in the Mesozoic, the Mosasaurs.

Ichthyosaurs were reptiles that had evolved into streamlined, fish-like forms. Many varieties inhabited the ancient seas. Strangely, most of them bore a close resemblance to the dolphins, which in time to come would replace them in the order of things. Ichthyosaurs were similar to dolphins and whales in another way. Unlike most of the dinosaurs, Ichthyosaurs did not lay eggs but gave birth to live young. Most Ichthyosaurs measured 2 to 3 metres (7 to 10 feet) long, the largest known specimen reaching 9 metres (30 feet). They attained their evolutionary peak in the Jurassic period 140 million years ago, and became extinct prior to the end of the Cretaceous. This seems a strange outcome for an animal so well equipped for survival; one apparently better adapted to its environment than some of the other creatures that lived on until the end of the Cretaceous, such as the Plesiosaurs.

During the Mesozoic Era, many forms of Plesiosaurs evolved. They were highly successful animals, a group that adapted in many ways to survive and thrive in the ancient seas. Many had extremely long necks, in some cases disproportionately so. The long-necked Plesiosaurs hunted fish in the surface waters of the oceans. Other marine reptiles, including several kinds of short-necked Plesiosaurs, dived to great depths to feed on squid-like animals. The short-necked Plesiosaurs or Pliosaurs usually had huge mouths, so they probably often killed large prey as easy targets, such as shellfish.

One Pliosaur became the largest of all marine reptiles. This was Kronosaurus. Reaching a length of over 12 metres (40 feet) with a skull that measured almost 3 metres (10 feet), Kronosaurus was the nearest thing to a whale that lived in the sea at that time.

The third group of reptiles that became marine predators were the Mosasaurs. These huge lizards, adapted by evolution for a life at sea, appeared towards the end of the Cretaceous period. Their jaws, armed with many long and extremely strong teeth, must have put the Mosasaurs among the fiercest of hunters in the ancient seas.

Whilst Ichthyosaurs, Plesiosaurs and Mosasaurs ruled the ancient oceans, their kingdom was shared by many other creatures. Some of them were not unlike animals familiar to us today, such as turtles and crocodiles. Archelon is the name given to a species of turtle which swam in the warm shallow seas of the late Cretaceous.

Although quite similar to the marine turtles of today, their ancient ancestors grew to be giants 4 metres (13 feet) long. Even so, these huge turtles may have fallen prey to the enormous crocodiles of the time, which used to hunt in the lagoons and along the shores of those prehistoric oceans. These were places that turtles, then as now, would have come in order to lay their eggs in the warm sandy beaches, way above high-water mark.

Ichthyosaurs and Plesiosaurs inhabited the Jurassic seas.

The ancient skies

It was during the Triassic period that reptiles launched themselves into a new dimension. They took to the air. At first they were gliders or parachutists, using wings of stretched skin just to float from tree to tree.

By the Jurassic, a group of animals with the power of true flight had evolved—the Pterosaurs.

Although Pterosaurs first solved the problem of flight, they were not the ancestors of the birds. Birds evolved separately from other dinosaurs, and had to await the extinction of the first masters of the ancient skies

before they were able to call it their own. Like birds, Pterosaurs evolved from reptilian ancestors. But also like birds, they were warm-blooded and, regardless of their ancestry, were therefore not reptiles. Recent discoveries of fossilized remains prove that, like mammals, fur often covered the Pterosaurs' bodies, even the undersides of the wings. Reptiles have smooth skins or scales, and fur is a most unreptile-like characteristic. Pterosaurs came in many sizes. Some were as small as sparrows. Others were the size of small aircraft, with wingspans as much as 10 metres (33 feet) across. Pterosaurs increased in size with the passage of time and with the evolutionary refinement of their body designs. The last of the Pterosaurs, those of the late Cretaceous, were the largest creatures that have ever flown—but they still met the same fate as all other dinosaurs.

Pterodactylus was a small Pterosaur of the late Jurassic. Only 22 centimetres (9 inches) long, it was tiny in comparison with many of the species yet to come. Pterodactylus resembled a medium-large bat with a long tooth-filled beak. It probably lived in colonies, roosting bat-like in trees or on sea cliffs. Its diet may have been made up of insects such as dragonflies, or small fish snatched from the surface waters along the seashore.

One of the most-studied Pterosaurs is called Pteranodon, a large animal with a wingspan of some 7 metres (23 feet). The location of many of its fossilized remains show that Pteranodon must have been a creature

Pterosaurs mastered the art of flying.

*The head of a
Pteranodon.*

that inhabited the coasts. It glided out over the ocean in the manner of today's albatross, scooping fish from the surface of the sea with its long pelican-like beak. The purpose of the crest mounted on Pteranodon's head remains a feature of speculation, but one thing is certain about its legs—they were almost useless. Movement on land must therefore have been extremely limited and difficult, proving Pteranodon to be an animal adapted for a predominantly airborne existence, a master of the late Cretaceous sky.

As the Mesozoic Era closed, birds were already living alongside the Pterosaurs. Archaeopteryx was the first known bird and, like the first Pterosaur, was more a glider than a flier. However, when the extinction of the dinosaurs was complete, birds had already evolved into many different forms. Owls and waders, gulls and herons succeeded where the Pterosaurs failed. And not only did they survive, they flourished.

The ancient land

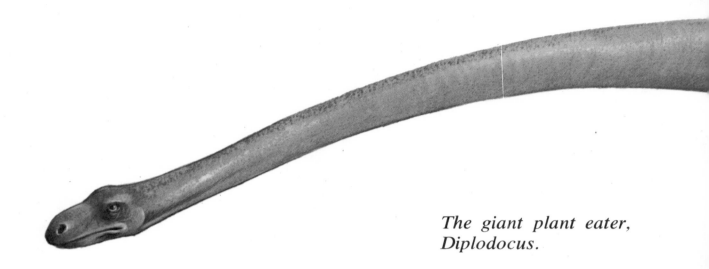

The giant plant eater, Diplodocus.

By the Jurassic period, dinosaurs had evolved that were the largest animals ever to walk the earth. One of these monsters was Diplodocus, a huge dinosaur that inhabited swamps and lagoons, where it fed on the abundant vegetation. It was in such areas that many of the largest dinosaurs lived. The warm climate of the time made the ancient land into a good provider of food, and the dinosaurs needed plenty of it to fuel their huge bodies. Diplodocus, for example, was almost 30 metres (100 feet) long. Diplodocus probably spent most of its time eating soft water plants as it waded around in the marshes. Its vast frame, mostly neck and tail, was controlled by a tiny brain set inside a very small head. Doing anything much more than eating would have been beyond the capacity of its rabbit-sized brain. Diplodocus spent its time in and around wet places probably in much the same way as the modern hippopotamus. Some scientists believe that it and most other large plant-eating dinosaurs were amphibious, at home both on land and in water. Others think that they roamed the forests like elephants.

Apatosaurus, once called Brontosaurus, also lived in similar areas to Diplodocus. But Apatosaurus weighed three times as much, and as a consequence this huge dinosaur probably spent most of its life in the water. Here it could take some of the weight off its enormous feet as the water helped support its 30-tonne bulk. Although Apatosaurus was heavier than Diplodocus, it was not as long. The tail was not as thin at the end, and the neck was more massive.

Fossilized footprints show that Apatosaurus did sometimes leave the water and walk on shore. This was probably to find a secure site in which to lay its eggs or move to new feeding grounds. On these occasions, the dinosaurs may have 'migrated' in herds much like wild elephants of today.

The largest of the dinosaurs that we yet know of was Brachiosaurus. A giant creature weighing as much as 100 tonnes and standing more than 12 metres (40 feet) high, Brachiosaurus could wade into fairly deep water in order to escape predators. This retreat in the face of danger was apparently the only protective measure that Brachiosaurus could take, having no other obvious means of defence. However, its awe-inspiring size may well have deterred all but the most ravenous of hunters.

It was during the Jurassic period that the giant plant-eating dinosaurs, the Sauropods, dominated the world's lowlands. As time progressed, these gigantic beasts of the swamps and river plains became scarcer. Their decline allowed other dinosaurs to fill the places they vacated. So even though some giant Sauropods did survive to the end of the Mesozoic, their heyday came and went in the middle of the Era.

Brachiosaurus, largest of land animals.

Apatosaurus, once called Brontosaurus,
a 30-tonne swamp dweller of the late Jurassic.

Another amazing inhabitant of the Jurassic landscape was Stegosaurus. Although not the largest, this dinosaur was certainly one of the most wierd-looking of the vegetarian dinosaurs. Stegosaurus grew to 9 metres (30 feet) long, and his almost 2-tonne bulk was under the command of a walnut-sized brain. Stegosaurus needed little brain power. With its back protected by a double row of bony plates and its tail armed with four vicious spikes, Stegosaurus only had to concentrate on eating most of the time.

The back-plates of this dinosaur have been a source of disagreement among palaeontologists for some time. One school of thought has it that the plates were purely and simply defensive shields that were held upright in the skin of the back. Another says they were held out at right-angles to the body, thus providing extra protective cover. A more recent theory is that they were used to dissipate excess heat, for the plates were in fact hollow and may have been filled with blood vessels. Blood passing through the large thin plates would have been efficiently air cooled. This is a good point to ponder, as Stegosaurus would have spent an awful lot of time grazing in warm sunshine and getting hot. Unlike the Sauropods, Stegosaurus does not appear to have been amphibious and therefore could not have taken to the water in order to cool down. The answer to the puzzle may well be something from each theory, the plates serving several purposes.

The controversial Stegosaurus.

When the huge Sauropods were lumbering through the lush swamp-lands and the plate-backed Stegosaurs grazed on the rich Jurassic undergrowth, some smaller dinosaurs were establishing themselves. One was Compsognathus, the smallest of the dinosaurs. It was only the size of a chicken and was very bird-like in its structure. It fed on flesh, not plant food, hunting for insects and lizards. Compsognathus was a Theropod, which means that it was a carnivorous dinosaur and ran about on two legs. So too did Coelurus, a flesh eater on a slightly larger scale, being some two metres (six feet six inches) long. Coelurus was probably quite swift-footed, being able to run down many of the primitive birds of the time as well as smaller dinosaurs and reptiles.

These Theropods were not the only dinosaurs to walk on their hind legs, but they did belong to a group which diversified into many types. Being carnivorous, they gave rise to the most fearsome killers of the Era. Another animal type to arise from the two-legged Theropod dinosaurs was Archaeopteryx, the first bird.

Compsognathus, a dinosaur of the late Jurassic.

When the huge plant-eating dinosaurs developed during the Jurassic period, nature also built predators to match. Great flesh eaters also developed to prey upon them. However, in the same period a cousin of the small flesh eaters was also developing in a way that, unlike the terrible hunters, would ensure its survival beyond the age of the dinosaurs. This was a small dinosaur destined to become one of the most famous of ancient life forms—Archaeopteryx. Its unique development was not in size but in its lifestyle, for it took to the air. This was because its scales had evolved into a covering of nature's most remarkable creations —feathers. But although Archaeopteryx had feathers, it did not have the power of true flight. Fossil records show no evidence of large flight muscles, and the air spaces that exist in the bones of modern birds to make them light were also absent. So this little feather-covered dinosaur was a glider, not a flier, but it was the first bird nevertheless. The wings of Archaeopteryx carried the same number of feathers as modern birds, giving its successors the ability to fly. Yet this first bird had not developed the other main bird feature, a true beak. Its reptilian head still had jaws that were full of teeth.

When these first birds appeared, the skies belonged to the Pterosaurs, and so the woodlands became their home. Here they did not have to compete with the great flying reptiles. They could survive among the trees until nature in time equipped them to take fully to the air and challenge the Pterosaurs.

The swift two-legged dinosaur, Coelurus.

When a Pterosaur became grounded, its puny legs made it extremely difficult to move around; in such situations, it became a prime target for predators. This was not true of the first birds for they could run and glide, making them highly efficient animals able to exploit two habitats, the land and the air. Most of their time, however, was probably spent in the trees hunting small lizards and insects.

In order to help them clamber about in the branches, they had three claws on each wing. This feature is shown in only one bird of modern times, the hoatzin of the tropical rain forests of South America. It is only the hoatzin chicks that have clawed wings similar to those of Archaeopteryx. They clamber about the branches around the nest shortly after birth, clinging with their feet and their ancestral wing claws. Hoatzins give us a real life glimpse into those distant times of 140 million years ago, when the reptile-like ancestors of all birds inhabited the Jurassic woodlands.

The hoatzin adult and chick.

Archaeopteryx glided through the sunlit glades of Jurassic forests.

During the Jurassic period, many varieties of plant-eating dinosaurs evolved, and they were preyed upon by an equally varied range of flesh-eating scavengers and hunters. One of the largest of these was Allosaurus, a dinosaur that stood on its hind legs. Its great feet were armed with huge hooked claws, as were its small front legs or arms. Allosaurus was most probably a slow-moving creature in comparison to the swift-running Coelurus, but it was fast compared to its huge, lumbering Sauropod prey. Weighing two tonnes, Allosaurus was a great killing machine, 11 metres (36 feet) long. Its huge jaws, full of teeth, enabled it to rip the flesh off its prey, much needed to fuel its own massive bulk.

Some of the animals that made up the prey of Allosaurus weighed 80 tonnes or more. They must therefore have been slow-moving creatures, and their hunter must have been able to catch them with ease on the ancient mud flats. Such encounters have been preserved in the form of fossilized footprints, even though they took place millions of years ago. The clawed feet of the hunter left their distinctive marks behind those of the gigantic Sauropod, whose prints look like dustbin-sized holes in the ancient riverside mud. The mud became sunbaked and hardened into rock, eventually to give silent witness to a life-or-death chase on the edge of the primeval swamp.

Once the great killer had brought down his prey, he may well have had to eat quickly and defend his catch against hordes or packs of other wandering predators. Allosaurus could have used his long stiff tail to sweep them aside while feeding, for doubtless a large kill would have attracted scavengers. Smaller dinosaurs may have gathered like modern-day jackals, awaiting their chance to run in quickly and carry off chunks of meat as Allosaurus fed.

The skull of the giant flesh-eating Allosaurus contained only a tiny brain.

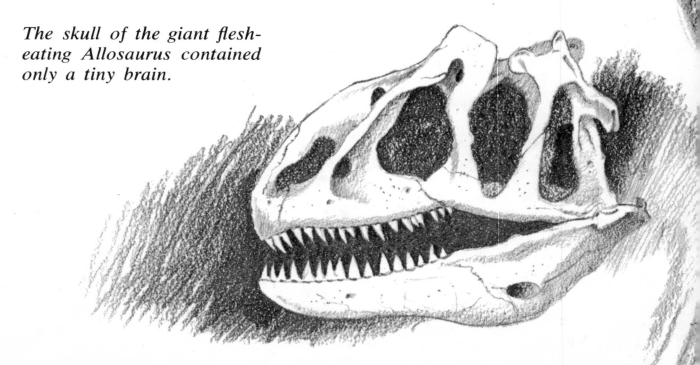

Coelurus may have been such an opportunist, using the fingers of his forearms as well as his jaws to snatch a piece from the colossal corpse. After feeding to its full, Allosaurus would have wandered off to find some quiet hiding place in which to rest up and digest its enormous meal—in much the same way as lions do today.

Not all the large two-legged dinosaurs were carnivorous and some, such as Iguanodon, lived upon vegetation. In 1878, the fossilized remains of a whole herd of these dinosaurs were excavated from a Belgian coal mine. The location and position of these remains showed that the Iguanodons had fallen into an ancient chasm. Perhaps they were frightened by a predator and stampeded, or the sudden crash of a thunderstorm made them panic and run, only to fall to their deaths in the rock-strewn ravine.

An Iguanodon stood up to 5 metres (16 feet) high and was approximately 11 metres (36 feet) long. Weighing as much as 4½ tonnes, it was a powerfully built but apparently peaceful giant. It had very large and powerful hind legs, and its much shorter arms were equipped with a bony spike in place of a thumb. The purpose of this device is still a mystery. Like the plates of the Stegosaurus, it could have had several uses. Perhaps it was a defensive weapon, or it may have been used to cut through the tough outer parts of some plants to get at the juicy insides.

Ouranosaurus, a sail-backed dinosaur. Its remains were found in the Sahara desert.

The plant-eating Iguanodon, so named because its teeth resembled those of modern iguanas.

Whatever its use, it was certainly not what was once thought. In 1851, the remains of several Iguanodons were pieced together and put on exhibition. What we now know to be a 'spiky thumb' was then mounted on top of the snout, making Iguanodon look rather like a rhinoceros. Subsequent discoveries of course proved this to be nonsense.

However, we must not laugh at the Victorians for this incorrect assumption, as it is sometimes very difficult to give correct answers in the absence of obvious clues. Consider for a moment, an elephant. If this had been an animal that became extinct with the dinosaurs, leaving no evidence behind except its bones, then the problem of describing the appearance, purpose and size of the trunk from the few clues left behind on the skull would be great indeed. If we had no similar living creatures with which we could draw a parallel, then we would probably not realize that the elephant had a trunk at all.

The science of palaeontology is one that is constantly searching for and finding new answers to old problems, and one that asks new questions about new discoveries. Among such new discoveries are the bones of a creature now called Ouranosaurus, unearthed in 1975. This animal, basically similar in construction to Iguanodon, had a series of rib-like bones sticking out from the spine. Like Iguanodon, this creature was found to be a plant eater, even though its remains were discovered in the area that is now the Sahara desert. In the days of Ouranosaurus, the Sahara was well covered in vegetation, but it was still a very warm region.

The bones could well have been the supporting ribs of a sail-like membrane that was raised along its back. The purpose of this sail was probably to dissipate body heat, and so prevent overheating while grazing during the hot day. However, few other dinosaurs ever developed such a feature, even though they too often lived in warm places.

One of the first dinosaurs to become known to science was discovered in 1822 and named Megalosaurus, which means giant lizard. This species, like its close relation Allosaurus, was a flesh eater and it too ran on two huge back legs armed with massive claws. The front legs or arms were also clawed, but small in comparison. Megalosaurus was not as large as Allosaurus, but at 9 metres (30 feet) in length, it was by no means a puny specimen.

The body design of creatures such as Megalosaurus must have been successful, for it culminated in the truly gigantic Theropod dinosaur called Tyrannosaurus rex. Last but greatest in the line of two-legged predators, Tyrannosaurus reigned supreme up to the very end of the dinosaurs' time on earth.

Largest of all known dinosaur hunters, Tyrannosaurus rex was an awesome creature. Standing 5 metres (16 feet) tall with jaws full of dagger-like teeth, this animal must have struck fear into all who came across it. The 10-tonne frame, 15 metres (50 feet) long, was carried along by two huge, cruelly clawed back legs. The forelimbs or arms were very small, only measuring 75 centimetres (2½ feet), and each ended in two clawed fingers, which must have been virtually useless in combat.

Megalosaurus, a flesh eater of the early Cretaceous.

Tyrannosaurus rex, the most renowned of predatory dinosaurs.

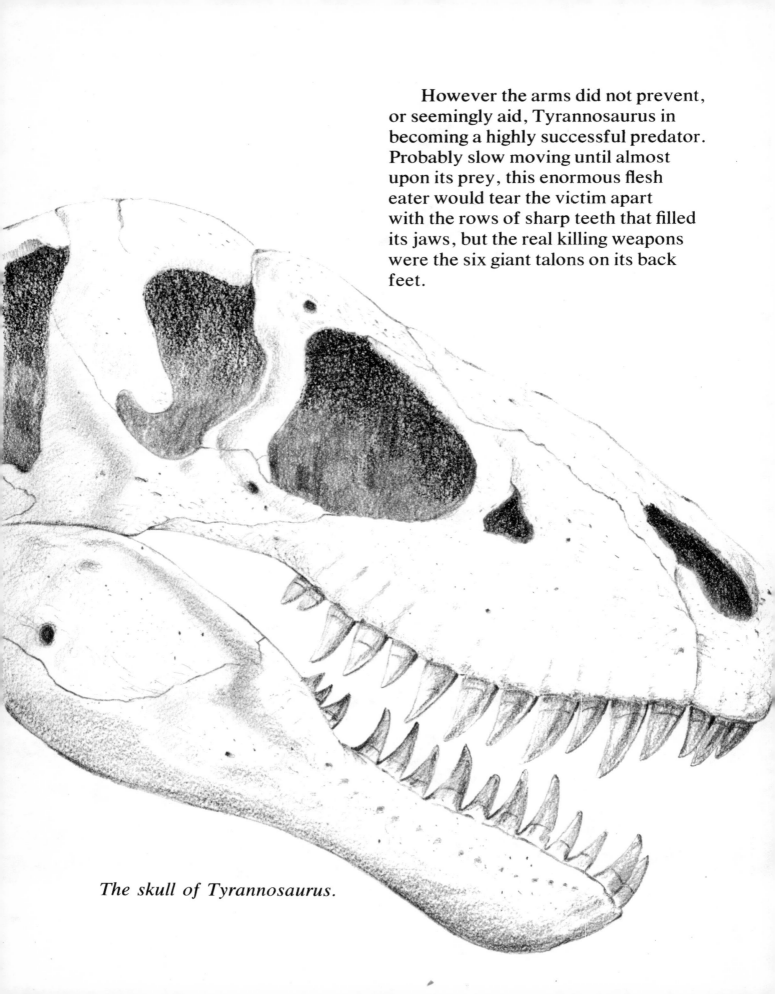

However the arms did not prevent, or seemingly aid, Tyrannosaurus in becoming a highly successful predator. Probably slow moving until almost upon its prey, this enormous flesh eater would tear the victim apart with the rows of sharp teeth that filled its jaws, but the real killing weapons were the six giant talons on its back feet.

The skull of Tyrannosaurus.

Apart from being a killer, Tyrannosaurus was also probably a scavenger like Allosaurus, feeding on the carcasses of dead Sauropods. The broken teeth of such predators have often been found among the fossilized bones of their prey. Such losses however were easily replaced, for one advantage that these dinosaurs had over the mammals was that they constantly replaced worn or broken teeth with new ones.

After gorging itself, Tyrannosaurus would have rested for quite some time. When so doing it may well have lain upon its belly, tail outstretched and its massive neck and jaw resting on the ground. This would help the dinosaur's digestive system to absorb its enormous meal. After such a rest, an opportunity to use the otherwise useless forelimbs could have occurred. On rising, Tyrannosaurus probably first braced its small arms against the ground, for strangely it did have massive shoulder muscles. When the hind legs flexed to rise, the arms stopped the body from sliding forward. The head would then have been tossed back, and the dinosaur rose to an upright posture.

Another use for the two-clawed arms could well have been to clean out the many teeth after feeding. We may well never be sure of their purpose, but one thing is certain; regardless of its strange appendages, Tyrannosaurus rex was the mightiest of the Mesozoic hunters.

These pictures show how large two-legged dinosaurs regained an upright stance after resting.

Another group of dinosaurs which, in the main, also used to stand on their hind legs in the same way as Tyrannosaurus, were the Hadrosaurs or duck-billed dinosaurs. They belonged to a most successful but diverse order, which also contained the Iguanodons.

Most Hadrosaurs were medium-sized dinosaurs. They weighed about 3 tonnes and measured some 9 metres (30 feet) long. The most distinctive feature that these dinosaurs developed was the rounded and flattened jaw that gave the group its odd name of duck-billed. The Hadrosaurs' teeth were also rather special. They evolved into perfect tools with which to deal with the many new plants of the Cretaceous period. The teeth lined the duck-billed jaw in many rows, in order that they could grind and chew almost any form of vegetation, even the most tough and fibrous.

At the end of the Cretaceous, many Hadrosaurs developed peculiar and ornate crests. This is Parasaurolophus.

Studies of the skulls of many Hadrosaurs have shown that they had a very acute sense of smell, and that their eyesight must also have been excellent.

One of the most interesting discoveries was a Hadrosaur skull in which the delicate bones of the ear were still intact. It shows that at least the Hadrosaurs, if not all dinosaurs, had perfectly good hearing. It would therefore seem to follow that dinosaurs could also communicate with one another by sound. Their many cries could well have rung out and echoed through the lush countryside of the Cretaceous period. Many of the voices would have belonged to the Hadrosaurs, as they constantly searched for food. The bellows, grunts and calls enabled the family groups or herds to keep in touch as they browsed in the thick cover of those long-dead forests.

While the various kinds of Hadrosaur skulls show that these dinosaurs

fed on land plants, their skeletons show an ability to swim. The long flattened tails and webbed hands and feet show that these land feeders must often have taken to the water, perhaps spending much of their early life there. They probably moved into the woodlands to live when mature, but even then retreated to the water when danger threatened, for swimming was beyond the capability of most Cretaceous predators.

One of the best known Hadrosaurs is called Anatosaurus, which was a large animal about the same size as Iguanodon. Anatosaurus was probably as much at ease running or walking on all fours as it was standing on its hind legs, for both front and back limbs had small hooves. The fact that Anatosaurus could move around in different ways depending upon the type of land, that it could also swim, and that it had keen senses of smell, hearing and sight, must have made it a very successful animal.

Related to Anatosaurus and possessing all the virtues of its relatives was a dinosaur that also developed a fantastic adornment. This is Parasaurolophus. On this dinosaur's head was mounted a crest 2 metres (6½ feet) long. The precise purpose of this strange structure, which was hollow, is still a matter of discussion and disagreement among scientists.

Parasaurolophus was not alone in developing a peculiar crest, as many other Hadrosaurs did so. In fact, scientists split Hadrosaurs into three

Anatosaurus, one of the duck-billed dinosaurs. Its remains are frequently found in North America.

main groups on the basis of their crests, so that this most diverse animal family can be better understood. We have flat-headed Hadrosaurs such as Anatosaurus, solid-crested animals, and hollow-crested dinosaurs like

Parasaurolophus. Each and every kind is one of nature's finest creations, superbly equipped and adapted for life—but all died out when the dinosaurs' mysterious end came and left no living relatives.

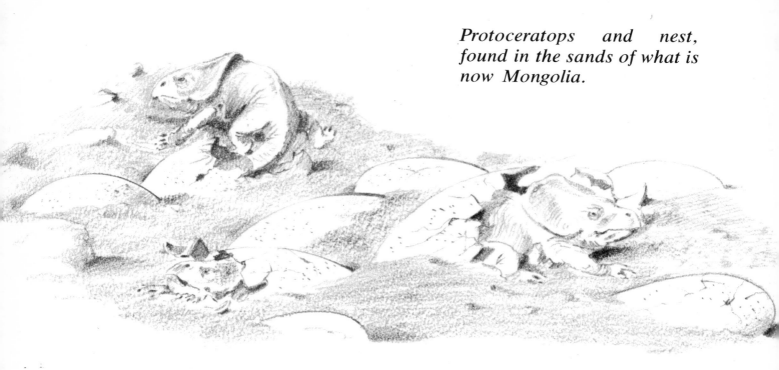

Protoceratops and nest, found in the sands of what is now Mongolia.

One of the last groups of dinosaurs to evolve were the Ceratopsians, which seem to have had a common ancestor in the armour-helmeted creature called Protoceratops.

Ceratopsians were horned dinosaurs that were able to defend themselves with some vigour. These rhinos of the past belonged to a long line of animals that evolved throughout the Cretaceous, culminating in the $8\frac{1}{2}$-tonne Triceratops.

These tank-like vegetarians, 8 metres (26 feet) long, probably roamed in small herds grazing on open pastures, secure in the knowledge that they were safe from almost any attack. But they could well have been as unpredictable as their modern counterpart the rhinoceros, charging at anything that seemed to offer a threat. Few animals could withstand a high-speed impact from an animal twice the size of an elephant and armed with three huge horns each a metre (yard) long. Should an attacker still be able to retaliate, Triceratops was protected by a huge horny shield that could deflect the slashing blows of a heavy clawed foot, the chief weapon of most predators.

While Triceratops is the most well-known Ceratopsian, other kinds had become widespread in the rapid evolutionary expansion of the Cretaceous period. Each variety had its own particular versions of horns and neck shield. Styracosaurus, shown in conflict with Tyrannosaurus on the covers of this book, was an early form of Cretaceous Ceratopsian. Its neck frill, rimmed by a series of horny spikes, was the most elaborate possessed by the group known as the short-frilled Ceratopsians.

Another dinosaur known as Torosaurus was last in the line of long-frilled types. Living towards the end of the age of dinosaurs, Torosaurus had a bony neck frill that extended over its back almost to the hind

The skull of Triceratops.

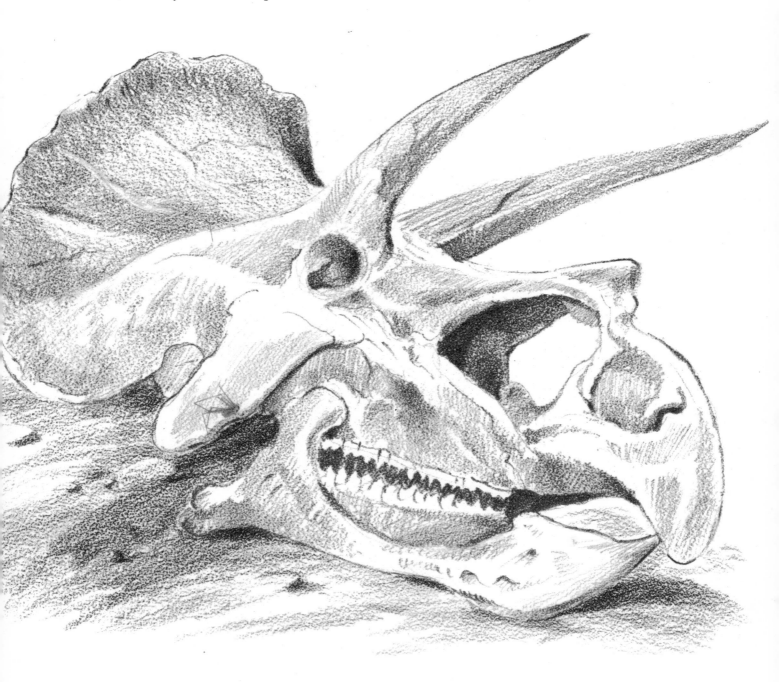

quarters, as well as possessing two long and doubtless lethal horns.

One thing that all Ceratopsians had in common was that their huge heads held teeth which could cut through the tough fronds of palms and other plants of the time. Also, their mouths terminated in a horny parrot-like beak driven by immensely strong jaw muscles, which could slice through the most resilient of growths. These dinosaurs could therefore feed on plants denied to other species that were less well equipped.

In the case of Triceratops, the power of the jaws came from the banks of jaw muscles more than a metre (yard) long. This, coupled with the fact that it could push over most trees to get at and eat the otherwise inaccessible foliage, ensured that this formidable animal was always well fed.

While the breeding methods of some dinosaurs may be a matter for speculation, we do know that Ceratopsians laid eggs. This fact was proved when a fossilized Protoceratops nest was unearthed in Mongolia. It contained both eggs and hatchling dinosaurs, newly emerged from the 7 centimetre (3 inch) shells.

Triceratops, the largest horned dinosaur.

A group of plant-eating dinosaurs called the Ankylosaurs developed during the Cretaceous, and they became armour-plated in order to ensure their survival. Stegosaurs began to decline in number at this time, 135 million years ago. Their place was taken by the Ankylosaurs, which expanded rapidly to fill the vacancy. These dinosaurs took their name from an animal called Ankylosaurus, recently renamed Euoplocephalus. It was 5 metres (16 feet) long, weighed some 3 tonnes, and its back was covered in thick bony plates as was its head. These grew out of the skin in the same way as the plates of Stegosaurus before it, but instead of having a spiked tail like its predecessor, Euoplocephalus had a huge bone lump, which converted the tail into a massive club or mace.

Although ponderous and slow-moving, the Ankylosaurs developed extraordinary coats of armour, finding this a successful formula for survival in the days of the most ferocious hunters. Scolosaurus was a huge animal covered in spikes. Even the tail carried two huge horns, which probably deterred predators from mounting an attack at all.

Another Ankylosaur called Palaeoscincus had horny spikes sticking out on all sides around a back covering of thick horny plates. This animal was probably the most heavily armoured of all dinosaurs. Its low, crouching posture kept the unprotected belly close to the ground, presenting only a huge array of indestructible armour plate and weaponry to an enemy. To kill such an animal, the attacker would have had to turn it upside down in order to get at the soft underbelly. In the attempt, it would have to endure the blows of the horn-tipped tail, driven by the muscle power of a 4- or 5-tonne creature desperately fighting for its life.

Scolosaurus, one of the most formidably armoured beasts of all time.

A modern animal that is rather similar to the Ankylosaur is the armadillo. This armour-covered mammal of South America also has a covering of thick plates, but it does not have to rely entirely on its bony armour for protection. Nature has also provided it with the ability to roll into a ball when attacked, thereby protecting its softer underparts. This is an example of convergent evolution, where nature solves the same problem for entirely different animals in the same way. It's a pity that the huge armoured Ankylosaurs did not have the ability to roll into a ball, for their fossils are often found upside down. Some predators obviously braved the lashing club-like tails, and heaved over the great tank-like creatures onto their back. Rendered helpless and incapable of quickly regaining their feet, they would have been easy prey.

All the Ankylosaurs seem to have fed in much the same way as tortoises, living entirely on plants. Unlike tortoises, however, they did have small teeth to help grind and break up tough plants, once they had cut through the fronds or stems with the sharp edges of their horny mouths.

Ankylosaurus, or Euoplocephalus, a fortress of the Mesozoic world.

Sail-backed dinosaurs may represent only a small percentage of the many types of dinosaurs, but they are among the most extraordinary. The peculiar sail, mounted along the backs of creatures such as Ouranosaurus and Spinosaurus, had been used by nature on other creatures that had appeared millions of years before. They became extinct long before dinosaurs evolved. Ouranosaurus has been mentioned before on page 40, and probably the purpose of the sail was to lose body heat in hot surroundings. However, the other user of this cooling system was a different type of creature.

Spinosaurus was a large flesh eater, its skin-covered sail towering almost 2 metres (6½ feet) above its back. While its back legs were much like those of the two-legged dinosaurs, its front legs were also quite large and Spinosaurus must often have walked on all fours. This posture, which requires less energy than walking on two legs, was probably its usual stance when searching for prey. Spinosaurus may well have only raised itself up when it attacked, launching its 12 metre (40 feet) long bulk against its herbivorous counterpart, Ouranosaurus. For both inhabited the same hot areas of land in the Cretaceous period.

A sail-back radiator was only one of many strange features that helped dinosaurs to survive. An equally peculiar adaptation belonged to a flesh eater called Deinonychus. This predator, 2 metres (6½ feet) in length, possessed an outsized sickle-shaped claw on each of its long back legs. These vicious devices could be swung back off the ground when walking, thus preserving the points in prime condition. The fossil records show that this fairly small dinosaur was capable of running swiftly and then leaping upon its prey. Thereupon, the long killing claws would have swung into action, impaling and even disembowelling the hapless victim.

The sail-backed predator, Spinosaurus.

The tail of this fierce flesh eater was very long and stiff, acting as a balance when running at speed in much the same way as the cheetah now uses its tail when hunting antelopes on the African plains. The stiff rod-like tail probably also helped to balance Deinonychus as it stood on one leg and slashed away at its victims with the other. When brought down, the prey would have been quickly killed by the heavily-toothed jaws and the hands, which were also equipped with large claws. Surely then, Deinonychus must have been the most ferocious, death-dealing creature of its age.

Deinonychus was a small but swift killer, one of the deadliest of all dinosaurs.

The use of a long stiff tail as a balance was also developed in a dinosaur called Hypsilophodon. Probably the swiftest of all dinosaurs, the 1½ metre (5 feet) long Hypsilophodon could have outrun even the terrible claws of Deinonychus. Weighing only 67 kg (148 lbs) and feeding on fruits, leaves and other vegetation, this small creature roamed the Cretaceous grasslands in the same way as the antelopes of today. It was also capable of evading its enemies in the manner of antelopes by leaping, twisting, turning and making off at high speed.

The back of this nimble dinosaur carried small bony plates in long rows, hinting that it evolved from some armour-backed ancestor. Hypsilophodon was a highly successful dinosaur. It remained unchanged for 100 million years, and then shared the same fate as all of its kind.

Another swift-running creature of the age of dinosaurs was the ostrich-like Ornithomimus, which means 'bird imitator'. A little larger than the ostrich of today, Ornithomimus was similar in that it ran on long back legs and possessed a long neck. It is a remarkable example of convergent evolution—of similar creatures evolving in similar conditions.

The most obvious visual differences between this dinosaur and the modern ostrich are the lack of feathers, the long tail, and arms

Ornithomimus

instead of the ostrich's useless wings. The fingers were capable of grasping the various items that formed its diet. Anything was eaten from lizards to fruit, a wide-ranging diet remarkably like that of the ostrich.

Like many of the swift-footed dinosaurs, Ornithomimus lived out the whole Cretaceous period, only to expire suddenly at the end of the age. Birds, mammals, insects, reptiles, and fish all shared the world with dinosaurs. Yet for some inexplicable reason they are all part of the animal world today while the dinosaurs, the most magnificent beasts of their time, are not. Dinosaurs became extinct, leaving us with no living example of their kind . . . or did they?

Rumour and legend have it that monsters still lurk in dark waters and remote places today. Serious and persistent investigation may yet reveal a creature that has survived the fate allocated to all its relatives—a living specimen from the amazing world of dinosaurs.

Agile and swift, Hypsilophodon was a common creature of the prehistoric plains and scrublands.

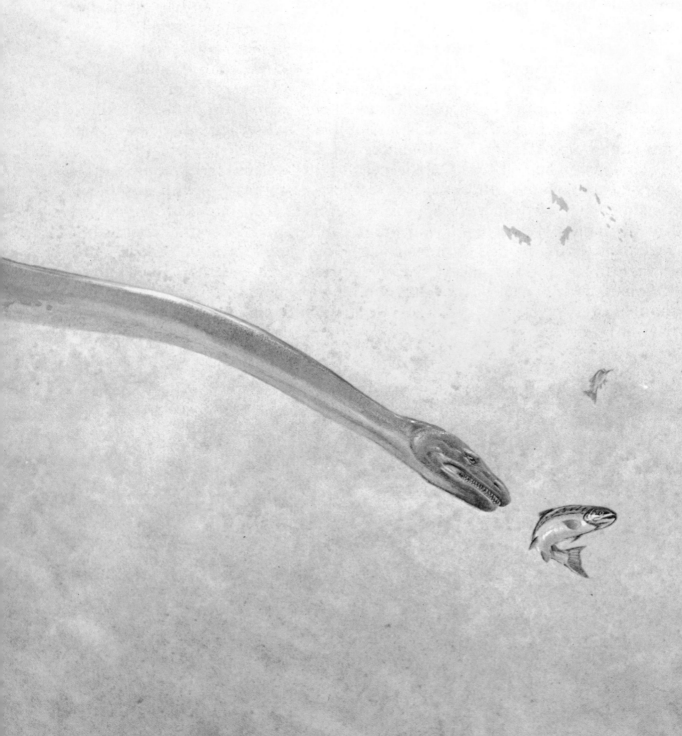

A Plesiosaur. Is this the elusive 'monster' of places like Loch Ness?

MONSTERS FROM THE PAST

As far as we know, all the dinosaurs became extinct about 65 million years ago, and none has survived to the present day. However, other animals that were once thought to have died out millions of years ago have been rediscovered, alive and well. Legends and sightings do suggest that large creatures, unknown to science, may be living in the lakes and seas of our modern world. Nature still has many mysteries, and only reveals her secrets if we pursue them with persistence and an open mind.

The rediscovery of an extinct creature obviously causes a great stir. Just such an event was the finding of a live coelacanth, which was an inhabitant of the seas when dinosaurs ruled the world. This primitive fish, like the dinosaurs, was thought to have been extinct for some 65 million years. Miraculously, it splashed and flopped its way back into our world in the net of an African fisherman on the 22nd of December, 1938. The specimen weighed 60 kg (132 lbs), measured 1½ metres (3 feet) long, and its body was covered in large blue scales. Comparison with fossilized specimens showed that these ancient creatures had remained unchanged for 300 million years, hidden in the ocean depths. Since this coelacanth was accidentally hauled to the surface, more than fifty have been caught. In fact, investigations among fishermen around the East African island of Anjouan showed that coelacanths were often caught there, and were not thought of as being peculiar at all. Other such living links with the distant past have been discovered in the ageless sea. Their arrival has not been

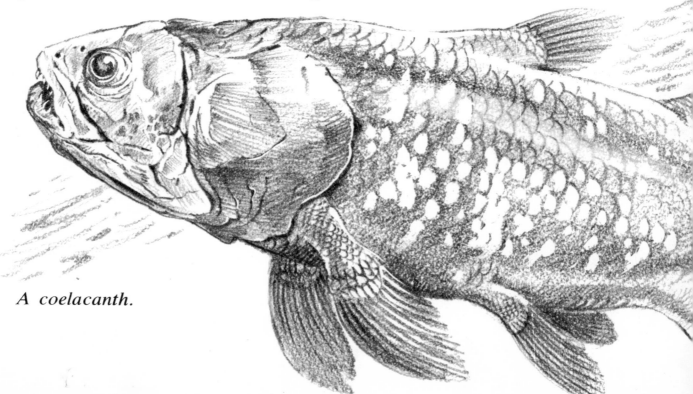

A coelacanth.

met with the same publicity as the coelacanths, because perhaps their physical appearance and size have not been as dramatic.

Today, there are many people who insist that they have seen huge 'monsters' in seas and lakes throughout the world. The most famous place for such sightings is probably Loch Ness in Scotland. The descriptions given by such observers of the 'monster' seen there often coincide with the likely appearance of a Plesiosaur, the extinct reptile of the Mesozoic seas. Shadowy photographs alleged to be of the Loch Ness monster do show a Plesiosaur-like creature. The 'return' of the coelacanth to the modern world from the distant past shows that we cannot totally ignore such evidence. So the mystery remains – does a Scottish loch harbour an unknown animal? Do the stories of 'sea monsters' hold a grain of truth? Do the deep dark waters of the oceans and lakes still hold the last of the giant reptiles?

The search continues, and we may yet be surprised and amazed by future discoveries.

Hutchinsoniella, a tiny crustacean discovered in 1954. This resident of eastern American coastal waters is related to creatures that inhabited the sea 500 million years ago.

Marine iguanas inhabit the Galapagos Islands in the Pacific Ocean.

ARE DINOSAURS ALIVE AND WELL?

Some scientists now think that the dinosaurs may not all have been cold-blooded animals like today's reptiles. In fact, as studies continue, more and more weight is given to the argument that quite a number of dinosaurs were warm-blooded. This alters some of the reasons put forward for their extinction, but it does not alter the fact that extinction did occur, and in a fairly short period of time. Compared with the long history of the world, the dinosaurs disappeared overnight. And, unless some survivor is found in the deep unchanging oceans and lakes, they would seem to be gone for ever . . . or are they?

While the dinosaurs vanished from the face of the earth, other creatures lived on. Many evolved into other shapes and forms, flourishing and advancing as they took advantage of the places vacated by the dinosaurs. Other animals were unaffected by the catastrophy, and did not find that the world was in any way a different place than before. They survived unchanged and, like the coelacanth, are still with us as living relics of the past.

Among the survivors from the
days of the dinosaurs are several
creatures that may give us a clue as to
the true appearance in life of many of
their long-dead companions.

Whether or not the dinosaurs were
cold-blooded reptiles, the most

dinosaur-like of today's animals do belong to this group of creatures. They include the crocodiles, which have changed little since their ancestors, the Archosaurs, thrived during the age of dinosaurs. And there are the strange marine iguanas, the sea-going lizards of the Galapagos Islands, which look fearsome but are content to graze on seaweed at the islands' shores.

On an island in the Indian Ocean lives a ferocious creature that may well resemble a dinosaur. This is the Komodo dragon, largest of living lizards. It is a predatory animal, and will kill creatures as large as goats. Not only can this 3 metre (10 feet) long lizard kill goats and small deer, but its mouth is large enough to swallow them whole. When running, the Komodo dragon extends its legs, so that the huge body is lifted off the ground. This voracious creature is then capable of a fast turn of speed.

The Komodo dragon, largest of living lizards.

Another animal giving us a similar link with the past is the tuatara, a lizard-like reptile of the Triassic period that has somehow survived unchanged. Although the tuatara's continued existence is now threatened by man's activities, it clings to survival on tiny offshore islands south of New Zealand. Untouched by time, little altered by evolution, these reptiles are the last living members of an ancient animal order older even than the dinosaurs. They endure the chill of their sea-mist shrouded islands, a far cry from the balmy days of the Cretaceous, but hibernate in winter, using the empty nesting burrows of seabirds. Even when the birds return, the tuataras do not move out. Nor are they required to do so, for the birds and the reptiles share the burrows in harmony. This association between these two survivors of a bygone age has lasted millions of years.

A tuatara, the living fossil that survived the dinosaurs.

So, dinosaur-like creatures continue to live on in the modern world, but what of the direct descendants of the dinosaurs—the animals that managed to evolve and survive the catastrophe that vanquished their forebears? They exist and thrive, are warm-blooded, and in fact are all around us—they are the birds. Archaeopteryx, the first bird, was the direct descendant of small, flesh-eating dinosaurs that lived in the Jurassic period. Since those distant times, when the birds witnessed the passing of the Pterosaurs, so gaining control of the skies, they have exploited every available habitat. From the ice caps to the tropics, from the deserts to the mountain tops—even the oceans became theirs. So then, some dinosaurs are alive and well, and we don't have to await the discovery of a 'monster' to prove it. They sing in our gardens; we keep them in cages; we eat their eggs. The amazing world of dinosaurs is still with us.

Some representatives from the world of dinosaurs as they are today: tortoise, birds, chameleon, crocodile.